Seymour Simon

BABY ANIMALS

SeaStar Books · San Francisco

This book is dedicated to Chloe and Jeremy.

Special thanks to reading consultant Dr. Linda B. Gambrell, Director of the School of Education at Clemson University, past president of the National Reading Conference, and past board member of the International Reading Association.

Permission to use the following photographs is gratefully acknowledged:
front cover: © Manoj Shah/Tony Stone Images; title page: © Tim Davis/Tony Stone Images; pages 2–3: © Stephen J. Krasemann, Photo Researchers, Inc.; pages 4–5: © Alan & Sandy Carey, Photo Researchers, Inc.; pages 6–7: © Nigel J. Dennis, Photo Researchers, Inc.; pages 8–11: © Tim Davis, Photo Researchers, Inc.; pages 12–13: © Bonnie Sue, Photo Researchers, Inc.; pages 14–15: © Brandon D. Cole; pages 16–17: © Mitch Reardon, Photo Researchers, Inc.; pages 18–19: © Kenneth H. Thomas, Photo Researchers, Inc.; pages 20–21: © Renee Lynn, Photo Researchers, Inc.; pages 22–23: © George and Judy Manna, Photo Researchers, Inc.; pages 24–25: © Tom & Pat Leeson, Photo Researchers, Inc.; pages 26–27: © Jim Merli, Visuals Unlimited; pages 28–29: © Jeff Lepore, Photo Researchers, Inc.; pages 30–31: © E. R. Degginger, Photo Researchers, Inc.; page 32: © Gary Randall, FPG International.

SeaStar is an imprint of Chronicle Books, LLC.

Library of Congress Cataloging-in-Publication Data is available.

Distributed in Canada by Raincoast Books
9050 Shaughnessy Street, Vancouver, British Columbia V6P 6E5

10 9 8 7 6 5 4 3

Chronicle Books LLC
85 Second Street, San Francisco, California 94105

www.chroniclekids.com

Baby animals live all over the world.

A baby horse is called a foal.

Right after a foal is born
it tries to stand on its feet.

In an hour it can walk around.

By the next day a foal can
run and kick its hooves
in the air.

A mother lion gives birth to
two or three cubs at one time.
The newborn cubs weigh
about three pounds each.
The mother feeds them
milk and little bits of meat.
By the time the cubs
are a year old,
they are hunting
with older lions.

A baby chick hatches from
an egg laid by a mother hen.
Chicks eat grain and seeds.
But chicks have no teeth.
So they swallow tiny stones
to help grind up their food.

Baby pigs are called piglets.

They will gain more than

200 pounds in just six months.

Piglets like to roll in the mud.

The mud keeps them cool.

A baby cow is called a calf.
Calves drink milk from
their mothers.

When they grow up they eat grass or hay.

A humpback whale baby
is also called a calf.
It is 12 feet long at birth.

In one day the calf drinks

100 gallons of milk

and gains 200 pounds.

A rhino calf weighs
over 100 pounds at birth.
It begins to eat grass, leaves,
and bushes at one week old.

Mother rhinos weigh
over 2,000 pounds.
That's as much as
20 baby rhinos.

Right after they hatch
from eggs, ducklings follow
the first moving thing they see.
Usually ducklings follow
their own mother.
But if they see you first,
they will follow you instead.

Puppies are born
blind and deaf.
But they begin to see
and hear after a week
or ten days.
A puppy's sense of smell
is over 100 times better
than a person's.

Like puppies, kittens are born blind and deaf and unable to stand.
After three weeks, they can see, hear, and walk. They play at hunting and catching.
After eight to ten weeks, kittens can take care of themselves without their mother's help.

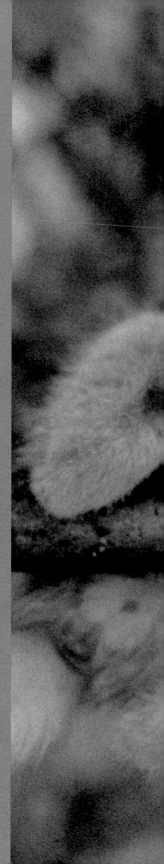

Eagle parents protect
their eggs in a nest
until they hatch.

The nest is built of sticks and may weigh 1,000 pounds or more. Baby eagles grow to be the size of their parents in just two years.

A mother garter snake gives birth to 20 or more baby snakes.

Young garter snakes are about the size of a pencil.

Mother snakes do not take care of their babies.

The babies start to hunt for worms, frogs, and fish as soon as they are born.

Baby deer are called fawns.

Fawns are not often seen.

They hide quietly

in tall grass or in bushes.

Their light-spotted brown

fur blends in well with

the leaves and twigs.

Baby rabbits are
also called fawns.
A mother rabbit has about
eight baby fawns at one time.
Each baby is only about
one inch long.
You could hold all of these
fawns together in your
two hands.

All over the world, baby animals are playing, growing, and learning how to survive.